"You mean a woman can open it...?"

THE WOMAN'S PLACE IN THE CLASSIC AGE OF ADVERTISING

Ad Nauseam

PRION IN ASSOCIATION WITH THE ADVERTISING ARCHIVES

First published in 1999 by
Prion Books Limited
Imperial Works
Perren Street
London NW5 3ED

ISBN 1-85375-351-3

All images courtesy of The Advertising Archives, London
Many thanks to Suzanne, Alison and Emma
Cover design by Bob Eames
Printed and bound in China
by Leo Paper Products Ltd

Woman's Delight!

THE "DALLI" BOX IRON.

The "Dalli is the most up-to-date and best Box Iron, doing away with the worries of the old system. No gas, no fire, no smell. Hot in a few minutes, and remains hot No changes of irons, self-heating with smokeless fuel. Can be used anywhere without interruption, even out of doors, doing double the work in half the time More economical than any other iron. Price of the "Dalli" is **6/-**. Price of the "Dalli" Fuel is **1/9** per box of 128 Blocks To be had of all Ironmongers or Domestic Stores. If any difficulty apply to—**The Dalli Smokeless Fuel Co., 27, Milton St., London, E.C.**

Ad Nauseam

"YOU MEAN A WOMAN CAN OPEN IT . . . ?" – THE WOMAN'S PLACE IN THE CLASSIC AGE OF ADVERTISING
Prion Books Ltd. Imperial Works, Perren Street, London NW5 3ED

The Dalli box iron – "Woman's Delight" **(1902)**

image courtesy of The Advertising Archives

Would your husband marry you again?

FORTUNATE is the woman who can answer "Yes." But many a woman, if she is honest with herself, is forced to be in doubt—after that she pays stricter attention to her personal attractions.

A radiant skin, glowing and healthy, is more than a "sign" of youth. It *is* youth. And any woman can enjoy it.

Beauty's basis

is pure, mild, soothing soap. Never go to sleep without using it. Women should never overlook this all-important fact. The basis of beauty is a thoroughly clean skin. And the only way to it is soap.

There is no harm in cosmetics, or in powder or rouge, if you frequently remove them. Never leave them on overnight.

The skin contains countless glands and pores. These clog with oil, with dirt, with perspiration—with refuse from within and without.

The first requirement is to cleanse those pores. And soap alone can do that.

A costly mistake

Harsh, irritating soaps have led many women to omit soap. That is a costly mistake. A healthy, rosy, clear, smooth skin is a clean skin, first of all.

There is no need for irritating soap. Palmolive soothes and softens while it cleans. It contains palm and olive oils.

Force the lather into the pores by a gentle massage. Every touch is balmy. Then all the foreign matter comes out in the rinsing.

If your skin is very dry, use cold cream before and after washing.

No medicaments

Palmolive is just a soothing, cleansing soap. Its blandness comes through blending palm and olive oils. Nothing since the world began has proved so suitable for delicate complexions.

All its beneficial effects come through gentle, thorough cleaning. There are no medicaments. No drugs can do what Nature does when you aid her with this scientific Palmolive cleansing.

Millions of women get their envied complexions through the use of Palmolive soap.

The Palmolive Company, Milwaukee, U. S. A. The Palmolive Company of Canada, Limited, Toronto, Ont.

Volume and efficiency enable us to sell Palmolive for

10c

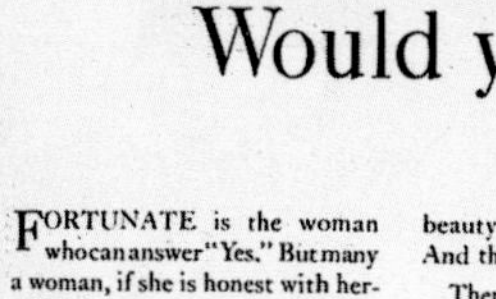

Palm and olive oils were royal cosmetics in the days of ancient Egypt

Ad Nauseam

"Would your husband marry you again?...fortunate is the woman who can answer 'Yes'" **(1921)**

image courtesy of The Advertising Archives

"YOU MEAN A WOMAN CAN OPEN IT...?" – THE WOMAN'S PLACE IN THE CLASSIC AGE OF ADVERTISING

Prion Books Ltd. Imperial Works, Perren Street, London NW5 3ED

Keep an eye on your wife

SOMETIMES appearance is deceiving. That's why we suggest that you keep an eye on your wife. Possibly she isn't as happy as she seems. Some time you may catch her when she's off guard and surprise a little wistful look on her face. Is she worrying about you? After all, most wives are loyal and proud, and rather reluctant to speak up. This may be miles from the fact —but there's a chance she's distressed because you aren't as careful about shaving as you were in times past.

Of course this suggestion is selfish on our part, but nevertheless a valuable hint. We urge you to be particular in the blade you choose and the way you use it. Today Gillette is offering a far superior razor blade. It makes frequent, close shaving comfortable and reasonably pleasant. Try it on our guarantee. Buy a package and use two blades. If you don't agree every shave is free from harshness and irritation—however tender your skin—return the package to your dealer and get your money back.

Gillette

RAZORS Gillette BLADES

"*Keep an eye on your wife*" **(1932)**

image courtesy of The Advertising Archives

"YOU MEAN A WOMAN CAN OPEN IT…?" – THE WOMAN'S PLACE IN THE CLASSIC AGE OF ADVERTISING

Prion Books Ltd. Imperial Works, Perren Street, London NW5 3ED

Ad Nauseam

"I CAN'T GO!.. I HAVE TO SCRUB MY FLOORS"

Can you imagine what the voice on the other end of the line is saying—when this intelligent woman admits she has to stay home to *scrub her floors*, instead of going out to have a good time?

Perhaps the friend, to avoid offence, only answers, "Oh, I'm sorry!" But the next time she sees this hard-working, hand-roughened floor scrubber, she will certainly remark, "For heaven's sake, why don't you use Johnson's Wax on your floors and furniture! You'll be an old scrubwoman at 40 if you don't stop this drudgery!"

Youth and beauty will stand just so much abuse. If you want *yours* to be preserved—while your floors and furniture are both beautified and protected with a minimum of effort—then use Johnson's Wax, and throw away your scrub bucket.

It's very simple. You first apply a very thin coat of the wax to your floors (wood or linoleum, varnished or unvarnished) with the longhandled wax applier. Let it dry thirty minutes, then polish with the Johnson Electric Polisher—which runs by itself, driving the wax deep into the pores. Thereafter, dust is removed in an instant with a dry mop. Worn spots renewed with a little wax on a cloth. And *no more scrubbing!*

For furniture, woodwork, leather and automobiles there is no polish or finish like Johnson's Wax. Its hard, dry film wards off stains, scratches, finger prints, smudges.

But be sure it's genuine Johnson's Wax—no substitute material can possibly give the same beauty and protection. On sale, liquid or paste, at hardware, grocery, drug or department stores. Dealers **RENT** out the Johnson Electric Polisher.

Send the coupon for a new free booklet—"Tragedy of the Young Scrubwoman."

SHI-NUP..FOR SILVER • A wonderful polish for silver, glass, enamel, nickel. At your store—made by S. C. Johnson & Son Inc.

JOHNSON DAILY RADIO GUIDE a new feature (over 50 coast-to-coast stations) tells every day what's on the air over your station.

S. C. JOHNSON & SON, INC., Dept. SP4, Racine, Wis. • Send me free your new booklet, "Tragedy of the Young Scrubwoman"—telling how to avoid scrubbing, how to use wax.

Name ______________________________

Address ______________________ City and State ______________________

"YOU MEAN A WOMAN CAN OPEN IT…?" – THE WOMAN'S PLACE IN THE CLASSIC AGE OF ADVERTISING
Prion Books Ltd. Imperial Works, Perren Street, London NW5 3ED

"Youth and beauty will stand just so much abuse" **(1932)**

"... Now you listen to Me!"

... I'm not complaining! ... I'm not nagging! ... I'm just telling you! ... I want $4.50 and I want it now!

● I've had just about enough of working 12-hour days while you're working 8—that is, if you don't take two hours for lunch ... I don't want more money—I want less work ... Look at your office—addressographs—adding machines—electric typewriters—extension phones—why, you don't even sharpen your pencils yourself ... You're working in 1934 in your business; I'm working back in 1920 ... That's why I want $4.50! ... I want just one home appliance that's going to lighten *my* work; that's going to shorten *my* day ... I want a New Hoover ... I'm sick and tired of pushing an Early American piece of electric cleaning apparatus around all day—struggling with it four times as long as I ought to, then not getting a tenth of the dirt. I want something that cleans *clean;* that cleans easier ... I want The Hoover! ... Come on, honey, let's have that $4.50 right now!

● Before replacing that old cleaner, be sure you see the new lightweight Hoover. MORE EFFICIENT: It cleans faster, easier, deeper. Removes not only dust and lint, but embedded grit. EXCLUSIVE PATENTED CLEANING ACTION: Positive Agitation, added to sweeping and suction. Vibrates rug, shakes loose deep-buried grit. NEW BEAUTY: Sentinel Series, streamline designs by famous stylists. FEATURES: Light weight; built-in Dirt Finder; new light duralumin Dusting Tools. PRESTIGE: Purchased by more people—3,250,000 in all. Endorsed by leading rug makers. SOLD ONLY THROUGH OUTSTANDING MERCHANTS: With bonded, trustworthy representatives in every neighborhood, who will gladly show you the new Hoovers when they call. HOME TRIAL: No obligation. THE FINEST CLEANER, YET ANYONE CAN OWN IT: Convenient terms; liberal allowance for old electric cleaners. Down payments as low as $4.50

The HOOVER

It LIGHTS ... As it Beats ... As it Sweeps ... As it Cleans

"...Now you listen to me!" **(1934)**

image courtesy of The Advertising Archives

Ad Nauseam

"YOU MEAN A WOMAN CAN OPEN IT...?" – THE WOMAN'S PLACE IN THE CLASSIC AGE OF ADVERTISING

Prion Books Ltd. Imperial Works, Perren Street, London NW5 3ED

A ROMANTIC MOMENT

Alone at last, the newly-weds pledge their love anew — undying, ever-faithful, etc., etc.

N. Y. Times Studio

HUBBY, DARLING, FROM NOW ON YOU GET A CEREAL THAT HAS FOOD VALUE
ANGEL WIFIE, IF IT DOESN'T HAVE FLAVOR I'LL GO STRAIGHT HOME TO MOTHER

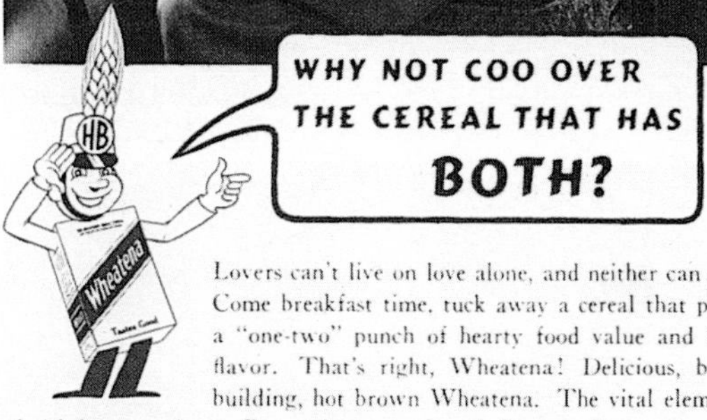

WHY NOT COO OVER THE CEREAL THAT HAS BOTH?
HB
Wheatena

Lovers can't live on love alone, and neither can you. Come breakfast time, tuck away a cereal that packs a "one-two" punch of hearty food value and high flavor. That's right, Wheatena! Delicious, body-building, hot brown Wheatena. The vital elements of rich brown wheat. Brown because wheat is brown. Fragrant, appetizing, tasting good because that wheat is roasted and toasted by an exclusive process. Don't be satisfied with a half-way cereal. Serve and enjoy the cereal with both food value and flavor—hot brown Wheatena.

Ad Nauseam

"Angel Wifie, if it doesn't have flavor I'll go straight home to mother" **(1937)**

image courtesy of The Advertising Archives

"YOU MEAN A WOMAN CAN OPEN IT…?" – THE WOMAN'S PLACE IN THE CLASSIC AGE OF ADVERTISING

Prion Books Ltd. Imperial Works, Perren Street, London NW5 3ED

Is the Joke on You?

Do you, too, wash curtains, covers, paintwork and windows—and find they won't *stay* clean long enough to let you rest? Then you must have noticed that the room hardest to keep clean is one where there's an old-fashioned smoky fire. *That* is where your dirt comes from. Soot and smuts! Thousands of tiny particles, too small to see, go floating round in the air and settling on everything. And when you realise that there is a lot of sticky tar in these smuts, you soon understand *why* your housework breaks your back.

STOP SCRUBBING SOOT! YOU can live in a cleaner, warmer house, have less to do, and save money. Simply heat *all* your rooms by gas and coke—the fires that *can't* make smuts. No need to give up your open fire. A glowing open *coke* fire is the most cheerful fire you've ever seen. Cheaper to run (saves 2d. in the 1/-); hotter; gas-ignited, which means NO paper, NO sticks, NO smoke—and NO smuts! Where you need quick heat, turned on and off with a flick, the answer is a gas fire. Lights with a flick. Very cheap to run. Ventilates the room while it burns. You can obtain the smartest new Gas and Coke fires on Easy Terms. *See your local GAS Showrooms about it.*

NO SMUTS! NO SMOKE!—WITH

GAS & COKE

Get this 2d. book FREE!

What does the Black Smoke Tax cost you? Why does the family spend 1/- more on washing bills in big towns than in small ones? Is yours a Gloom Baby or a Sunshine Baby? Do you live in Happiness House—or Heartbreak House? Ask for this astonishing, illustrated magazine-book, 'Britain's Burning Shame' (published price 2d.) FREE at your local Gas Showrooms to-day.

ISSUED BY THE BRITISH COMMERCIAL GAS ASSOCIATION, GAS INDUSTRY HOUSE, 1 GROSVENOR PLACE, LONDON, S.W

"Darling, you <u>do</u> work hard to keep our little home dirty!" **(1939)**

Ad Nauseam

"YOU MEAN A WOMAN CAN OPEN IT...?" – THE WOMAN'S PLACE IN THE CLASSIC AGE OF ADVERTISING

Prion Books Ltd. Imperial Works, Perren Street, London NW5 3ED

Good Cook, Good Housekeeper, Good Wife — *but she didn't know the first thing about shoes!*

'It's not my fault if my shoes get wet, old and out of shape! I've got to wear something. Look at these! New two months ago!'

'Yes, I remember the bill, and I can't afford any more!'

Then she learnt shoe-*chic*onomy

Ad Nauseam

"Good cook, good housekeeper, good wife – but she didn't know the first thing about shoes!" **(1939)**

image courtesy of The Advertising Archives

"YOU MEAN A WOMAN CAN OPEN IT…?" – THE WOMAN'S PLACE IN THE CLASSIC AGE OF ADVERTISING

Prion Books Ltd. Imperial Works, Perren Street, London NW5 3ED

Ad Nauseam

"YOU MEAN A WOMAN CAN OPEN IT…?" – THE WOMAN'S PLACE IN THE CLASSIC AGE OF ADVERTISING
Prion Books Ltd. Imperial Works, Perren Street, London NW5 3ED

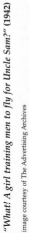

***"What! A girl training men to fly for Uncle Sam?"* (1942)**

image courtesy of The Advertising Archives

If men bought clothes the way women do!

But I always wear size 38!
I was only looking, thank you!
CLOTHIER
Are you sure I'll have this exclusively?
I'm returning these for credit!
ERNIE METZL

With all the sly fun poked at them, the ladies still have the last laugh. They always get their money's worth in style, in quality, in value. They adroitly choose the right dress made from the right fabric, for the right occasion...consistently demanding clothes made from fabrics bearing a name known and trusted — Pacific Mills.

It's a wise man who takes a tip from the ladies. Next time you buy, ask first for a suit in one of Pacific's specialty fabrics because it's been planned to serve your special needs. Clothes of Pacific specialty fabrics offer distinctive appearance and fine value at moderate cost. Pacific Mills, Worsted Division, New York.

LOOK TO THE *fabric* FIRST – BUY PACIFIC

Although demand still exceeds supply, leading stores the country over will soon be receiving increased quantities of clothes made from new Pacific specialty fabrics... including Plateau, *the suit with the weightless feel,* priced at $55; Surrëtwill, *the 4-in-1 suit,* at $40. And for hot weather wear, it's Mohara, *the cool tropical-plus-crisp appearance,* priced at $52. For further information address Pacific Mills, Worsted Division, Retail Service Bureau, 200 Fifth Avenue, New York 10.

Pacific Worsteds Woolens

"If men bought clothes the way women do!" **(1946)**

image courtesy of The Advertising Archives

"YOU MEAN A WOMAN CAN OPEN IT…?" – THE WOMAN'S PLACE IN THE CLASSIC AGE OF ADVERTISING
Prion Books Ltd. Imperial Works, Perren Street, London NW5 3ED

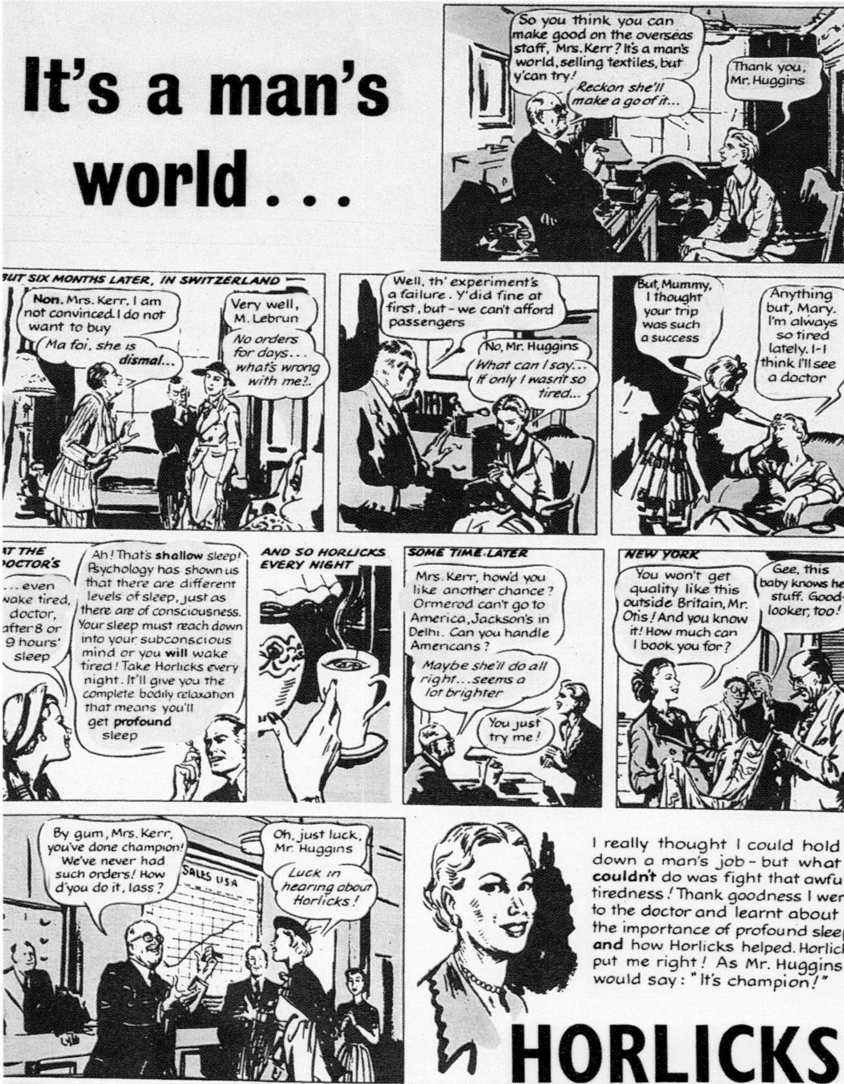

Registered at the G.P.O. as a Newspaper. Printed in Great Britain by SUN PRINTERS LIMITED, London and Watford, Herts, for the Proprietors and Publishers, HULTON PRESS, LTD., 43/44 Shoe Lane, London E.C.4. Sole agents for Australia and New Zealand, Gordon & Gotch (A sia), Ltd.; South Africa, Central News Agency, Ltd.; Sole agents for Israel, Pales Press Co., Ltd.

Ad Nauseam

"YOU MEAN A WOMAN CAN OPEN IT...?" – THE WOMAN'S PLACE IN THE CLASSIC AGE OF ADVERTISING

Prion Books Ltd. Imperial Works, Perren Street, London NW5 3ED

"It's a man's world selling textiles, but y'can try!" **(1951)**

image courtesy of The Advertising Archives

"THE WAY TO A MAN'S HEART"
Based upon the Creamola Technicolor Film—see it at your local cinema.
AREN'T men *beasts*. Listen to him! "Are you trying to poison me," indeed! After all the trouble she goes to, thinking up meals in these difficult days.
What's that? "Never darken my door again?" She's begging him to give her one more chance. But he's adamant. The man hasn't a heart!
Now what? Is she off to cookery classes? Ah, no, nothing so practical with this little innocent. She's wandering away in a dream.
Here she is, walking through the clouds of Space, and here's the world, looking very cheery as he takes what's coming to him from the Scots boy.
What *is* it the world's enjoying? Of course — "*Creamola* tickles the world's palate". Then it's one of the many delicious Creamola sweets, or. . . .
. . . CREAMOLA CUSTARD
RICH—SMOOTH—CREAMY
"WHY, HE HAS A HEART AFTER ALL!"
GET THE PACKET WHERE YOU SEE A PICTURE OF THE WORLD AND ME
CREAMOLA CUSTARD
CREAMOLA CUSTARD is made with the finest ingredients. It has a flavour of its own—try it, you'll like it better!

Ad Nauseam

"YOU MEAN A WOMAN CAN OPEN IT…?" – THE WOMAN'S PLACE IN THE CLASSIC AGE OF ADVERTISING

Prion Books Ltd. Imperial Works, Perren Street, London NW5 3ED

Aren't men beasts. Listen to him! "Are you trying to poison me," indeed! After all the trouble she goes to, thinking up meals in these difficult days **(1951)**

If your husband ever finds out
you're not "store-testing" for fresher coffee...
... if he discovers you're still taking chances on getting flat, stale coffee ... woe be unto you! For today there's a sure and certain way to test for freshness before you buy
REGULAR GRIND
PRESSURE PACKED
Chase & Sanborn
COFFEE
Here's how easy it is to be sure of fresher coffee
Look for the "Dome Top" Can of Chase & Sanborn. That firm, rounded top shows it's packed under pressure, fresh from the oven.
Just do this:
Press your thumbs against the dome top before you buy. If it's firm, it's fresh. If the top clicks, pressure's gone—take another. It's the one way to get the freshest coffee ever packed.
No other can lets you test!
You can't test an ordinary flat top can. Some are "leakers" that have let air in to steal freshness. But all flat top cans look alike. You can't tell which are good and which are stale.
Here's the payoff!
Sure as you pour a cup, they'll want more! For Chase & Sanborn is a glorious blend of more expensive coffees . . . brought to you fresher. No wonder Chase & Sanborn pays a flavor dividend you won't find in any other coffee!
"PRESSURE PACKED"
Chase & Sanborn

Ad Nauseam

"YOU MEAN A WOMAN CAN OPEN IT...?" – THE WOMAN'S PLACE IN THE CLASSIC AGE OF ADVERTISING

Prion Books Ltd. Imperial Works, Perren Street, London NW5 3ED

"If he discovers you're still taking chances on getting flat, stale coffee...woe be unto you!" **(1952)**

image courtesy of The Advertising Archives

Is it always illegal
TO KILL A WOMAN?

FOR SIX MONTHS I bend the ears of the home office to get a postage meter. I win . . . Then the only good, fast, dependable, honest-to-Gregg stenographer I got, this redhead Morissey—balks at a postage meter!

"I have no mechanical aptitude. Machines mix me up, kind of," she says. As if we asked her to fly a P-80. I almost blow my top.

This postage meter, I explain, is modern, more efficient, a time saver . . . No more adhesive stamps. No stamp box, and who's got the key? No running out of the stamps you need. No scrounging. No stamp sticking. Just set the lever for any kind of stamp you want, for any kind of mail, and the meter prints the stamp right on the envelope with a dated postmark—and it seals the flap at the same time. Faster than mailing by hand. Prints stamps on tape for parcel post. Will handle anything we have to mail out of this office. Even keeps its own records!

And metered mail doesn't have to be postmarked and cancelled in the postoffice, gets going earlier. It is practically heaven's gift to the working girl . . . and so on. But with the Morissey, no soap.

I TRY diplomacy. "Miss Morissey, I want you person'lly to try it for two weeks. If you don't like it then—back it goes to the factory! I depend on your judgment implicitly. Okay?" . . . She acts like an early Christian about to be lunch for a lion, but gives in.

So help me—two weeks later she has a big pink bow on the handle of the postage meter—like it was an orchid or something. I give it the gape.

"Kinda cute, ain't it," says Miss Morissey. "But a very efficient machine, Mr. Jones. Now the mail is out early enough so I get to the girls' room in time to hear all of the dirt" . . . I wonder is it always illegal to kill a woman!

WE ARE always learning some new advantages of the postage meter. If you'd like to learn what one could do for your office, call the nearest Pitney-Bowes office. Or write for an illustrated booklet.

PITNEY-BOWES *Postage Meter*

PITNEY-BOWES, Inc., 1125 Pacific Street, Stamford, Conn. *Originators of Metered Mail. Largest makers of mailing machines. Branches in 63 cities in the United States and Canada*

Ad Nauseam

"YOU MEAN A WOMAN CAN OPEN IT…?" – THE WOMAN'S PLACE IN THE CLASSIC AGE OF ADVERTISING

Prion Books Ltd. Imperial Works, Perren Street, London NW5 3ED

"Is it always illegal to kill a woman?" **(1953)**

You mean a <u>woman</u> can open it?

Easily—without a knife blade, a bottle opener, or even a husband! All it takes is a dainty grasp, an easy, two-finger twist—and the catsup is ready to pour.

We call this safe-sealing bottle cap the Alcoa HyTop. It is made of pure, food-loving Alcoa Aluminum. It spins off—and back on again—without muscle power because an exclusive Alcoa process tailors it to each bottle's threads after it is on the bottle. By vacuum sealing both top and sides, the HyTop gives purity a double guard.

You'll recognize the attractive, tractable HyTop when you see it on your grocer's shelf. It's long, it's white, it's grooved—and it's on the most famous and flavorful brands. Put the bottle that wears it in your basket . . . save fumbling, fuming and fingers at opening time with the most cooperative cap in the world—the Alcoa HyTop Closure.

Alcoa Aluminum

ALCOA

ALUMINUM COMPANY OF AMERICA

Pittsburgh, Pa.

Ad Nauseam

"YOU MEAN A WOMAN CAN OPEN IT…?" – THE WOMAN'S PLACE IN THE CLASSIC AGE OF ADVERTISING

Prion Books Ltd. Imperial Works, Perren Street, London NW5 3ED

"You mean a woman can open it…?" **(1953)**

"Not a man in sight..."

As I was driving along a country road with four other women as my guests a tire went flat. My heart sank with it, for my tire-changing experience was nil and the road was empty of aid. Pulling to the side, I hunted out the tools, remarking as I did so:

"Not a man in sight, of course. What we need is an angel from heaven!"

Imagine our astonishment when a cheery voice above our heads said, "I'll be down in a minute, lady." Unknowingly, I had stopped beside a telephone pole at the top of which sat our "angel"—a line repairman.

> *From the* Reader's Digest *feature*, Life in These United States . . . *"true stories showing appealing or humorous sidelights on the American scene."*

A Friend in Need

We got a chuckle out of that little story and we hope you did too. Best thing about it is that it isn't an isolated case.

Many a time each day, telephone men and women go out of their way to help someone in trouble. Their friendly, neighborly spirit is one of the nice things about telephone service.

BELL TELEPHONE SYSTEM

"Not a man in sight..." **(1955)**

image courtesy of The Advertising Archives

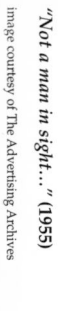

"YOU MEAN A WOMAN CAN OPEN IT...?" – THE WOMAN'S PLACE IN THE CLASSIC AGE OF ADVERTISING

Prion Books Ltd. Imperial Works, Perren Street, London NW5 3ED

Ad Nauseam

WHAT MAKES A PERFECT WOMAN?

Do you freeze with him at football matches? Brave the 'jalopy'—and *blow* your nylons? Suffer sock-darning with a smile? Good! You get 7 out of 10. Now go for full marks. (Easy!) Just give him a TERN. Definitely the gift he'll *adore* you for, every time he wears it. (You'll love him in it, too). *Wonderful* shirt. Never needs ironing. Always looks smart. Bliss for bachelors! Ready to give—with your love—for only **39/6.** In white, cream, blue, grey or green never-iron poplin. Buy him a TERN *today*.

CHRISTMAS TIME—TERN TIME

TERN

Trade Mark

by Consulate

NEVER-IRON POPLIN

M. Bertish & Co., Ltd. London, N.15.

"What makes a perfect woman?" **(1955)**

image courtesy of The Advertising Archives

Ad Nauseam

"YOU MEAN A WOMAN CAN OPEN IT...?" – THE WOMAN'S PLACE IN THE CLASSIC AGE OF ADVERTISING

Prion Books Ltd. Imperial Works, Perren Street, London NW5 3ED

LADIES!

HERE'S THE KEY TO YOUR L PROBLEMS

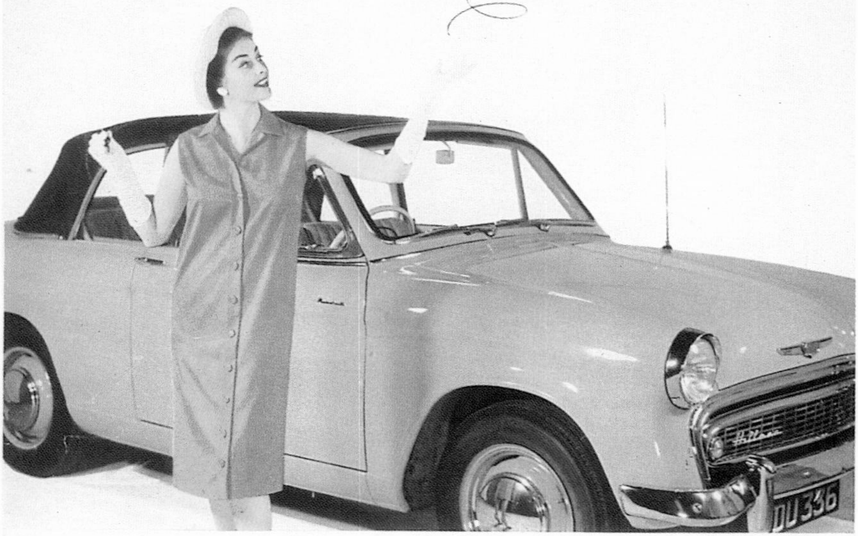

Dress by Fredrica. Hat by Otto Lucas, London

Get your Husband to buy a new car with

The Selective-Automatic

manumatic

REGD TRADE MARK

2 Pedal motoring at its best!

Send for this full colour catalogue which describes the joys of 2-pedal motoring.

AVAILABLE ON:

AUSTIN A55 · HILLMAN MINX · M.G. MAGNETTE · MORRIS OXFORD · WOLSELEY 15/50

DEPT. C · AUTOMOTIVE PRODUCTS CO. LTD · LEAMINGTON SPA · WARWICKSHIRE MI6

Ad Nauseam

"YOU MEAN A WOMAN CAN OPEN IT...?" – THE WOMAN'S PLACE IN THE CLASSIC AGE OF ADVERTISING

Prion Books Ltd. Imperial Works, Perren Street, London NW5 3ED

***"Ladies! Here's the key to your 'L' problems... 2 pedal motoring"* (1958)**

image courtesy of The Advertising Archives

LADIES' DEPT.

What she looks for—

- ✓ COMFORT AND ROOMINESS
- ✓ SMART GAY COLOURS
- ✓ REALLY LARGE LUGGAGE TRUNK
- ✓ EASILY ADJUSTABLE SEAT
- ✓ SENSIBLE DOORS—*safe for children*
- ✓ EASY GEAR CHANGE

MAINLY FOR MEN

What he insists on—

- MORE MILES PER GALLON—*up to 36 m.p.g.**
- GOOD ACCELERATION—*0-70 m.p.h. in 45 secs.**
- SAFE BRAKING—*no doubt about that!*
- VISIBILITY—*Excellent. Good demister too*
- EFFICIENT SPRINGING—*superb!*
- HANDLING—*what a joy!*

** The Autocar 25.10.57*

Together you'll choose a

Remember, too, Morris quality protects your investment—your Morris is always *worth more* in re-sale value. TWELVE MONTHS' WARRANTY—and backed by B.M.C. Service, the most comprehensive in Europe. Morris Owners planning a Continental Tour are invited to see their Morris dealers for details of a free service to save foreign currency.

"QUALITY FIRST"

MORRIS OXFORD

PRICES FROM £589 (Plus £295.17.0 Purchase Tax)

MORRIS MOTORS LTD., COWLEY, OXFORD. London Distributors: Morris House, Berkeley Square, W.1. Overseas Business: Nuffield Exports Ltd., Oxford, and 41-46, Piccadilly, London, W.1

8 12C

Ad Nauseam

"YOU MEAN A WOMAN CAN OPEN IT...?" – THE WOMAN'S PLACE IN THE CLASSIC AGE OF ADVERTISING
Prion Books Ltd. Imperial Works, Perren Street, London NW5 3ED

"What she looks for – smart gay colours...sensible doors" **(1958)**

image courtesy of The Advertising Archives

The Chef
does everything
but cook
– that's what
wives are for!

"Cooking's fun" says my wife "... food preparation is a bore! Think of the meals I'd cook you if I had a Kenwood Chef!" For the Chef beats, whisks and blends. With its attachments it liquidises, minces, chops, cuts. Slices, grinds, pulps. It shells peas and slices beans. Peels potatoes and root vegetables. Opens cans, grinds coffee. Extracts fruit and vegetable juices. It helps with *every* meal—from a welsh rarebit to a four-course dinner. I can take a hint—I'm giving my wife a Kenwood Chef right away!

▲ *The Kenwood Chef complete with three beaters, bowl and a big recipe and instruction book is yours for only 27½ gns. tax paid. (Easy terms are available.)*

JUST FOUR OF THE CHEF'S WONDERFUL ATTACHMENTS

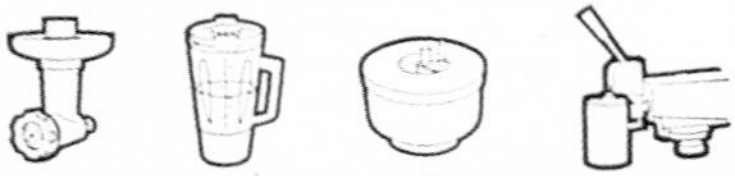

MINCER LIQUIDISER POTATO PEELER CAN OPENER

The Kenwood Chef has more attachments — DOES MORE JOBS FOR YOU — *than any other food preparing machine.*

Send off this coupon for a husband-persuading leaflet about the Kenwood Chef

NAME

ADDRESS

H W.30

Kenwood Manufacturing (Woking) Ltd., Old Woking, Surrey

WPS 199

I'm giving my wife a

Kenwood Chef

Ad Nauseam

"YOU MEAN A WOMAN CAN OPEN IT…?" – THE WOMAN'S PLACE IN THE CLASSIC AGE OF ADVERTISING

Prion Books Ltd. Imperial Works, Perren Street, London NW5 3ED

"The Chef does everything but cook – that's what wives are for!"
(1961)

image courtesy of The Advertising Archives

"To think I cook a meal while I'm typing!"

My mother used to worry so much about my not eating properly, ever since I left home and got a job—and my own flat.

She knew I always had sandwiches for lunch and she guessed I was lazy about cooking a proper evening meal when I got home at night.

She said she was going to give me a present for my flat—and suddenly, the cooker was there, all gleaming and modern-looking.

It was a fully-automatic electric cooker! And to christen it, my mother had prepared a meal and put it in the oven while I was at the office. Then she had to go back to the country. But she'd set the dials—

—and my supper was just ready and piping hot when I got home. Oh I did enjoy it! Now I prepare my supper myself, every morning. The dials are easy as pie to understand (I thought they wouldn't be)—

—and I've plenty of time in the morning because if I want a cooked breakfast the cooker does it overnight and has it ready just as the alarm clock goes off!

Apart from this wonderful automatic business I've fallen for electric cooking because it's so clean and quick. Costs so little to run, too.

Go to your Electricity Service Centre to choose your new cooker; they are all tested and approved and there is a good selection for you to see. They will also tell you about the *very* easy terms.

Get up to date go electric!

Issued by the Electrical Development Association

"To think I cook a meal while I'm typing!" **(1961)**

image courtesy of The Advertising Archives

"YOU MEAN A WOMAN CAN OPEN IT...?" – THE WOMAN'S PLACE IN THE CLASSIC AGE OF ADVERTISING

Prion Books Ltd. Imperial Works, Perren Street, London NW5 3ED

Be brave in distinctive new Chart Stripes from University Row®.

Chalk up another triumph for University Row Authentics! To bring out the tiger in you, smart stripes on white for dress wear. And this smooth-going Oxford shirt has all the University Row features you expect: contour-cut for a longer, leaner look; button-down collar; full pleat and loop in the back. Stripes in many basso-profundo colors such as Burgundy (shown), Bluebeard, and Black. Wear University Row Authentics in stripes and go, tiger! You'll have those kittens seeing stars — and stripes — forever! $5.95.

University Row
Manhattan®
The Dean of Authentic Styling

Ad Nauseam

"YOU MEAN A WOMAN CAN OPEN IT . . . ?" – THE WOMAN'S PLACE IN THE CLASSIC AGE OF ADVERTISING

Prion Books Ltd. Imperial Works, Perren Street, London NW5 3ED

"Go, tiger! You'll have those kittens seeing stars – and stripes – forever!" **(1966)**

image courtesy of The Advertising Archives

Get what you've always wanted
the great grooming action of a hair cream from a liquid.
If you haven't been getting all you want from a liquid hair groom, get new Score Liquid. Gives you the great grooming action of a cream. That's because new clear Score Liquid is made by the men who make clear Score Hair Cream. So you get great grooming action. And you also get Score's famous greaseless look, Score's famous masculine scent.
SCORE
LIQUID HAIR GROOM
a clear liquid with the grooming action of a cream
Score® Liquid Hair Groom
Score—Three Ways.™ Hair Cream. Spray Deodorant. Liquid Hair Groom.
©1967 Bristol-Myers Co.

Ad Nauseam

"YOU MEAN A WOMAN CAN OPEN IT...?" – THE WOMAN'S PLACE IN THE CLASSIC AGE OF ADVERTISING

Prion Books Ltd. Imperial Works, Perren Street, London NW5 3ED

"Get what you've always wanted – Score-Three Ways" **(1967)**

image courtesy of The Advertising Archives

Should a gentleman offer a Tiparillo to a dental hygienist?

"The doctor is a little late, sir. Will you have a seat?"

She's the best thing to hit dentistry since novocaine. "Hey Dummy," your mind says to you, "why didn't you have this toothache sooner?"

Maybe if…well, you could offer her a Tiparillo.® Or a Tiparillo M with menthol. An elegant, tipped cigar. Slim. And your offer would be cleverly psychological. (If she's a bit of a kook, she'll take it. If not, she'll be flattered that you *thought* she was a bit of a kook.) And who knows? Your next visit might be a house call.

Ad Nauseam

"YOU MEAN A WOMAN CAN OPEN IT…?" – THE WOMAN'S PLACE IN THE CLASSIC AGE OF ADVERTISING

Prion Books Ltd. Imperial Works, Perren Street, London NW5 3ED

"The doctor is a little late, sir. Will you have a seat?" **(1968)**

image courtesy of The Advertising Archives

If you guys don't buy
these new Drummond sweaters,
we'll go right back
to male models.

DRUMMOND

FROM $17 TO $35, IN LOTS OF COLORS; OF PURE WOOL, SUEDE AND WOOL, OR MOHAIR-AND-WOOL BLEND. AT GOOD STORES; OR WRITE DRUMMOND, EMPIRE STATE BUILDING, NEW YORK, N.Y. 10001.

Ad Nauseam

"YOU MEAN A WOMAN CAN OPEN IT…?" – THE WOMAN'S PLACE IN THE CLASSIC AGE OF ADVERTISING

Prion Books Ltd. Imperial Works, Perren Street, London NW5 3ED

"If you guys don't buy these new Drummond sweaters…" **(1968)**

Blow in her face and she'll follow you anywhere.
Hit her with tangy Tipalet Cherry. Or rich, grape-y Tipalet Burgundy. Or luscious Tipalet Blueberry. It's Wild! Tipalet. It's new. Different. Delicious in taste and in aroma. A puff in her direction and she'll follow you, anywhere. Oh yes . . . you get smoking satisfaction without inhaling smoke.
TIPALET
Cherry
TIPALET
Natural
TIPALET
Burgundy
TIPALET
Smokers of America, do yourself a flavor. Make your next cigarette a
Tipalet.
New from Muriel.
About 5 for 25¢.

Ad Nauseam

"YOU MEAN A WOMAN CAN OPEN IT…?" – THE WOMAN'S PLACE IN THE CLASSIC AGE OF ADVERTISING

Prion Books Ltd. Imperial Works, Perren Street, London NW5 3ED

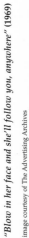

"Blow in her face and she'll follow you, anywhere" **(1969)**

85% of MG Midget owners are men.

Which means lots of girls will be relaxing in our new, thick contoured rake adjusting seats.

A scene we're sure will appeal to both driver and passenger.

As will the trendy new look. There's a new matt black recessed grille with chrome surround. New light clusters. Split rear bumpers. Black and silver Rostyle rally wheels. And round the sides you'll find black side-winders. For a long, lean look.

The MG Midget comes in four wild new colours. Glacier White, Blue Royale, Flame Red, and Bronze Yellow. And of course, you can still get Pale Primrose and British Racing Green.

Get switched on – and immediately you'll know why this is the enthusiasts' car. The famous race and rally proven twin-carb. engine performs brilliantly.

The MG Midget will give you dynamic acceleration. Magnificent high speed cruising. And economical fuel consumption.

We've given you all this (rake adjusting seats included) for £838*.
The girl you'll have to get for yourself.

* Recommended price including P.T. Extra is charged for delivery, seat belts, number plates, radio and aerial.

Sport the real thing. MG Midget.

Ad Nauseam

"YOU MEAN A WOMAN CAN OPEN IT...?" – THE WOMAN'S PLACE IN THE CLASSIC AGE OF ADVERTISING

Prion Books Ltd. Imperial Works, Perren Street, London NW5 3ED

"Lots of girls will be relaxing in our new, thick contoured rake adjusting seats. A scene we're sure will appeal" **(1969)**

image courtesy of The Advertising Archives

Undies to be sold in.
Not you? Don't bargain on it. The will of Allah could catch you in your undies any time.
Blushmaking? Not in Triumph fashion undies. Get in some quick. They're a great buy.
Triumph. Co-ordinating bras, bra-slips, briefs, pantie-girdles, mini-slips, waist-slips, mini-coats and nighties in the prettiest prints, plains and laces.
Buy them in sets or one at a time. Prices from only 9/11. Sizes 32-38.
Triumph. Undies to be seen in.
Triumph
INTERNATIONAL

"Undies to be sold in" **(1969)**

image courtesy of The Advertising Archives

Ad Nauseam

"YOU MEAN A WOMAN CAN OPEN IT…?" – THE WOMAN'S PLACE IN THE CLASSIC AGE OF ADVERTISING
Prion Books Ltd. Imperial Works, Perren Street, London NW5 3ED

The Mini Automatic. For simple driving.

Optional automatic transmission available on all models except G.T. and Cooper 'S'. Recommended price £97.18.4 (£97.92) inc. p.t.

The Mini automatic does one little thing more for you.

It changes gear without you changing gear. This little thing can make a world of difference in all kinds of driving conditions.

In congested traffic you don't fight a running battle with the gear stick. The gearbox fights its own battles.

When you're driving fast you keep both hands on the wheel all the time, which makes for a safer ride. And whenever you feel like a bit of fast armwork through the bends, you can switch from automatic to manual.

Then our automatic has some hidden benefits. You can't stall on the clutch because there's no clutch pedal to stall on.

You can't grind into the wrong gear because you don't change gear. In fact the Mini automatic is the closest thing you'll find to a built-in chauffeur.

It makes driving as effortless as sleeping. Sleeping, luv. You lie down, close your eyes and…

Mini

Mini: greatest invention since the wheel.

Ad Nauseam

"It makes driving as effortless as sleeping. Sleeping, luv. You lie down, close your eyes and..." **(1970)**

image courtesy of The Advertising Archives

"YOU MEAN A WOMAN CAN OPEN IT...?" – THE WOMAN'S PLACE IN THE CLASSIC AGE OF ADVERTISING

Prion Books Ltd. Imperial Works, Perren Street, London NW5 3ED

"There is no other purgatory but a woman." Beaumont and Fletcher
Yes, but what a way to go.
VIRGINIA SLIMS
MENTHOL FILTER
Warning: The Surgeon General Has Determined That Cigarette Smoking Is Dangerous to Your Health
VIRGINIA SLIMS
FILTER
VIRGINIA SLIMS.
You've come a long way, baby.
Regular & Menthol: 18 mg. "tar", 1.2 mg. nicotine av. per cigarette, FTC Report Nov. '70

"You've come a long way, baby" **(1972)**

image courtesy of The Advertising Archives

"YOU MEAN A WOMAN CAN OPEN IT…?" – THE WOMAN'S PLACE IN THE CLASSIC AGE OF ADVERTISING

Prion Books Ltd. Imperial Works, Perren Street, London NW5 3ED

Ad Nauseam